# SOLO
# PERFORMANCES

## Thirteen Monologues for Women

**Anne Barwood, Brian J. Burton,
Alfred J. Greenaway, Angela Lanyon
and Angeline Wilcox**

# HANBURY PLAYS

Keepers Lodge Broughton Green
Droitwich Worcestershire WR9 7EE

# SOLO PERFORMANCES

First published 2004
© Anne Barwood, Brian J. Burton, Angela Lanyon
Angeline Wilcox, Alfred J. Greenaway
ISBN:- 185205266X

## INDEX

# FOR WHOM PHONE RINGS
## Alfred J. Greenaway

It was Dulcie, the Vicar's wife, of all people, who got me into this. "Here you are" she said, "still a spinster of this parish, and not an eligible man in sight. Time you did something about it." I brushed it off with a laugh, saying I'm not bothered, but it started me thinking. I chose to be a career woman, and I've done reasonably well, but I do get this nagging feeling that it would be nice to have a man about the house if only to replace a bulb or mend a fuse. Then Dulcie comes up with the suggestion. "Have you ever considered a dating agency?" I can tell you, she's a goer for a vicar's wife! I was appalled. Think of the risks involved; all those lurid cases one reads about. You could be a bride in church one month and a bride in the bath the next. I pooh-poohed the whole idea - and yet here I am filling in a questionnaire from the *Friends for Life* agency, which Dulcie insists is a most respectable organisation. My brain must be softening. It's very difficult making a pen picture of oneself - and very revealing. You're tempted to write down "Intelligent." Then think there must be some doubt about that from the very fact that you're filling in the form. "Reliable" Yes, that's a plus. "Fond of the outdoors" - could give the impression that you'd prefer to live in a tent "Good Gardener" even that's slightly doubtful after that fiasco at last year's Horticultural Show. "Good Cook" - yes, I think I'd get away with that. My friends always complement me on my dinner parties. That's a good selling point Oh! What the hell! Why should I bother? *(Screws up form)* There are advantages in the single state - being your own mistress instead of someone else's. You don't have to account for your comings and goings - fewer responsibilities. And yet *(yawns)*. I think I'll have an early night - make myself a nice mug of hot chocolate and curl up in bed with a good book - and it won't be *Great Expectations!* ........................ *(Telephone rings)* Oh, that'll be Dulcie. She often rings about this time to give me a rundown on the local gossip. One must be aware of the day's events and keep abreast of the local gossip! *(Crosses DR to answer the telephone,)* ...... Celia Bravington ..... Who? ..... Geoffrey who?

... Geoffrey Hawkins? You're not selling double-glazing, are you?.... Do I remember a Geoffrey Hawkins? ... Oh, that Geoffrey! My goodness! It must be getting on for twenty years. How nice to hear from you after all this time. How are you? ... I'm fine too. You went to Australia, didn't you? ... You've come back for good - in spite of the British climate, and you're looking up old friends ... Of our circle, I think I'm the closest to Dulcie ... Yes, she married the local vicar... It's not all that funny, is it? I know she was a bit of a raver in her youth, but she's settled down now and become totally respectable. Overdoes it a bit, in fact, but there are flashes of the old Dulcie from time to time ... Yes, I hear from Samantha occasionally. According to her, she practically runs the Civil Service ... Tommy and Harriet? I get a Christmas card from them. They married and went to live in Sunderland - voluntarily, I believe. How about you? Did you marry? ... Me, neither. I suppose I've been too busy... It is pleasant to hear from you, Geoffrey, but we musn't overdo the nostalgia, must we? ... That's a very kind thought. I'd love to. There's quite a decent little restaurant here on the High Street. Do you like Italian food? ... At the Ritz? Are you serious... You're staying there?... My goodness, you must have made that fortune. Well, if you can afford to wine and dine your old friends at the Ritz, you certainly aren't on the breadline. This is really very kind - I'll be delighted... Wednesday at 7-30: I'll be there. I'm reliable if nothing else, Geoffrey. I look forward to our meeting, it should be great fun! ... Yes, 'bye for now, Geoffrey. *(She replaces the receiver)* I must be dreaming! Dinner at the Ritz with the handsome Geoffrey who's returned from Australia with a fortune. Keep your imagination in check, woman. An invitation to dinner is not a proposal of marriage. I expect he just wants to get firsthand information about his old friends. Still ... at the very least, dinner at the Ritz is not to be sneezed at .... I don't think this is the time for hot chocolate. I'll have a sherry instead - possibly two.

*(Exits L. humming "I'll see you again."*

# OUT OF THIS WORLD
## Brian J. Burton

Do you remember those halcyon days when we were kids, when the sun always shone during those long summer holidays, when friendships were forged and others broken? But, like all things, it had to come to and end and, like Shakespeare's schoolboy, at last we crept unwillingly back to school. And almost as soon as we'd settled back in and faced the inevitable, there came that request for an essay on "My favourite adventure during the summer holiday" or something of the kind. Do you remember that? You do? Well that's exactly what I'm going to do now - not write an essay but tell you about my favourite adventure during this long summer. There is one snag, though. You're not going to believe me. I know -it's so out of this world, you'll just laugh at my audacity for even thinking, for one moment, that you'll believe me. All the same, I'm going to tell you. - believe it or not. (*Casually*) I went to the moon - you know - that white globe up in the sky where the man grins down at us. There you are, you see I said you'd laugh, didn't I? Do you know how I got there? No, I wasn't a stowaway on the Moon Shuttle - that was years and years ago and I certainly didn't go on a package holiday - even that is outside the range of *Jules Verne Holidays*. (*Again casually*) I flew there on my own. No, no, no, no! I'm not a witch. I can' t ride a bicycle, let alone a broomstick. No - nothing like that. I just flew there under my own steam - if you understand what I mean. And, by the look on your faces, you haven't got a clue. Mind you, I was pretty tired by the time I got there - after all, it is a long way. But I got there in the end. The landing was much easier than I thought it was going to be - probably because I wasn't overloaded with luggage. I only took an overnight bag. I hadn't told any of my family where I was going in case they worried about me They might have done.. But, there I was on the moon. I was in for quite a surprise though. I hadn't really read much about those men who got there before me. I didn't exactly know what to expect. I'm a bit like that - take things as they come and all that. So, there I was sinking into the surface of the moon. It was like very soft sand and it was blue - the palest of blues you could imagine. Not only that but with every step I took, I shot up into the air like a rocket. Something to do with gravity, I suppose. I studied Arts rather than Science, so I suppose I should have done my homework before I left. But, after a while, I started to adjust to it and even enjoyed it, in a strange way - a bit like Disneyland, I suppose. So, I ploughed on - well, that's hardly the right expression - leapt on, I suppose, is a better way of describing it. Now, I don't know how far those first men on the moon ventured with their module - if that's what they called it - but either they didn't go as far as I did or they went the other way. (*Matter of fact*) I found a path - not surfaced or anything like that - but a definite road of some kind. In a very short time, it led to a sort of shop, at the side of the path, where a man was selling weighted boots - the kind that stop you from flying up in the air all the time. But that was where I met my first snag. I hadn't thought of bringing any money with me. Anyway, I don't suppose even Thomas Cook has lunar dollars, and the man in the shop wouldn't take plastic - well, you can understand that can't you? I didn't speak the language, of course, but I managed to convey my problem to him and, with surprising generosity, he gave me a pair. I wonder if these Moonmen are somehow related to the Aboriginals who used to give you anything of theirs you admired. I had absolutely no idea how to thank him. Do Moonmen shake hands or kiss or even rub noses, perhaps? So I smiled and bowed, like they do in the Orient, and he seemed to get the gist of my meaning. So things were a lot better from then onwards. I had found my feet, if you get my meaning. So I carried on along the path for a while, thinking that, if there were other men on the moon, apart from the shoemaker, they must have somewhere to live and so, with a bit of luck, I might find some sort of settlement.

I turned a corner and there was an incredible garden. All the flowers and trees where exactly the same as the flowers and trees back on earth but with one exception - they were all blue - flowers, branches, leaves, fruit - all blue. I resisted the temptation to pick the fruit and eat some, although I was getting very hungry. I had been too excited to think about breakfast before I left home and that was a long time ago -a few thousand miles, in fact. So, I stopped and marvelled and carried on along the path for a considerable way and then, turning another corner, I was,at once, confronted with an enormous lake - a vast stretch of the bluest water you could imagine, even in your wildest dreams. And, all round this lake., on the banks, were stalls - you know, like a French Market. And some of the things they were selling were just incredible - all kinds of food, household items - even animals and yes, you've guessed it, they were all blue. I wandered from stall to stall just gazing in amazement. They were all wonderful but the one that fascinated most of all was selling crystal - the most unbelievable blue crystal you could possibly imagine. - the depth of colour defied description. It seemed to echo the blue of the lake itself. Again, no money but, with a display of Lunar generosity, the old stall-keeper pressed a small piece of blue crystal into my hand and smiled. I put it into my jacket pocket and, after another bow carried on. But, by this time, I was starting to feel very, very tired - a sort of Lunar jet-lag, I suppose. So I made my way around the bay until I found a small cave where I could lie down and get some sleep. In no time at all, I was dead to the world - I supppose I should say I was dead to the moon. Anyway, I didn't wake up until my alarm clock went off. Yes, yes, you've guessed it - it was all a dream - but what a dream! I have a habit of cutting things fine - always have done, so I rushed into the bathroom, had a quick wash and rushed down stairs to grab a quick breakfast, picked up my jacket from the chair, where I must have thrown it before I went to bed, put my hand in my pocket to get my car keys and realised there was something strange in my pocket. I took it out and I stopped in my tracks. It was very small piece of blue crystal-the most magnificent piece of crystal in all the world. Well. I said you wouldn't believe me, didn't I? To tell you the truth, half of those holiday essays when I was at school were only partly true. Were yours? Come on - tell me - were they?

# CIRCLE DANCING

### Angela Lanyon

Now, come along everyone, it is the church fete, after all. We must show willing. Brian? Maureen? Oh, you're going to sit out. are you? Well, I should move the chair a bit. No, a bit further. Well away, Maureen, you remember what happened last week. No, Patsy, it wasn't your fault. I said so at the time. How many more times ... shut up, Julian. No, sorry, I didn't mean ... Oh, well if you're going to be like that. Now, come on, people, are we going to have a rehearsal or not? You know what the vicar said. Right? Yes, well this is a Greek dance. Yes, it's a circle dance so we all need to stand in a circle to start with. A bit further out, Patsy.... a circle, everyone. Now look round and see where everyone else is standing and shuffle along until you get your position right. Everyone ready? Now, we start with hands high and feet together. Facing inwards, Brian. Inwards. Yes, that's right. What is it, Maureen? Oh, you're going to do the music. Splendid. It's the tape with the blue spot. Side B. For goodness sake, Maureen, turn it down. And wait till I tell you when to start. Right, everyone, are we ready? Hands like this. Right foot to the right, bring the left up to it and stamp. Sorry, Julian, I didn't realise it was your foot. No, I wouldn't have stamped on it if it had been anyone else's. No, Julian, I didn't mean that - I do wish you'd try to be less touchy. Now, perhaps, if everyone moves apart a bit more. we can get on. No, Patsy, there is no need to go right over there. Yes, very well, if you're going to sneeze .... All right - be like that. No, we don't all want flu or the black death or whatever .. For goodness sake it's supposed to be a harvest dance not a riot. Oh, do come back, Patsy. Maureen, can we go back to the beginning? What? The tape's stuck. Well, just push "rewind." You have? All right, Brian, if you think you can fix it. And now, while we're waiting, Patsy, have you finished sneezing? For heaven's sake,unplug it first, Brian, if you're going to poke a nail file in the back. Yes, of course, it's insured. Yes, Kate, a good idea. Perhaps if we took our shoes off Did everyone hear what Kate said? While we're all waiting for Brian to fix the tape off, we'll all take our shoes off. Are you getting anywhere, Brian? Oh, good. Now we really must get started. A big circle, everyone - and do try to smile - we're supposed to be enjoying ourselves. A circle. The harvest's home and we're all celebrating. Hands high and right foot and left and - oh dear! Are you all right, Patsy? Yes, it does look a bit odd - sort of funny angle. Yes, Julian, you could be right, it might be broken, but let's just try and look on the bright side, shall we? Can you put your weight on it, dear? Yes, she has gone a bit pale, Maureen - a sort of nasty green colour. I don't think you'll be able to dance with a foot like that Perhaps you'd better sit down until the pain's gone off it a bit. What's that, Brian? You think you've got a connection? Splendid. You did remember to unplug it, Brian! Oh, dear! Is everyone all right? Maureen? Oh, there you are, Julian. Julian. can you look for the light switch .... Then you'd better see if you can find the door ... In the hall. Has anybody got a mobile? ... Oh, your coat's in the hall, is it? Well perhaps somebody .. Okay, Julian, then you'd better dial 999 - and Julian - don't take all day about it. And now, I suppose, I shall have to tell the vicar the dancing's off.

# JELLO AND CRACKERS
## Brian J. Burton

*A TABLE CENTRE STAGE WITH FOUR CHAIRS AROUND IT*
Here we are, Jason. We'll sit right here. You sit on that side and I'll
sit opposite you right here. Are you okay? You are? Good. Now,
isn't this just dandy - you taking your mother out to tea, just like a
big grown-up man? Now, just you mind you behave yourself this
time. I don't want to see you throwing bread at the waiter like you
did when we were on vacation down in San Diego in the fall ...
What's that, Jason? ... no, no, no, you cannot throw anything at
all at the waiter - no, nothing whatsoever ... no, not even a teeny
bitsy crumb. What do you mean? This waiter has not got bad
eyesight. I'm quite sure he's seen us. Look, he's putting some
glasses on that table over there ... No, sit down, Jason - we do not
need to move over to that table. We're swell right here. Just wait a
while and the waiter will be over in the flicker of an eyelid. Jason,
stop flickering your eyes like that. It won't make the waiter come
any sooner. You don't want people to think you're a silly boy, do
you? You do! I see Ah, here's the waiter right now. He's come to
take our order. You were so busy asking silly questions, you
haven't thought about what you want to order. What? You have
to think? Well, hurry up then and have a big, big think while I tell
the young man what I want. Okay? Sorry to keep you waiting, I
would like a flat white and a plate of chocolate cookies, please.
Thank you ..... Jason! You do not have to stand on your head to
think ... Yes, I'm sure it's mighty difficult .... No, no, I am not
going to try it myself - whatever next? ... No, and the waiter
doesn't want to try it either. Come back to the table this instant
... That's better. Now, sit up properly and try to behave like a
little gentleman. Now what would you like for your tea? .... What?
Now, don't be ridiculous .. Yes, I know it says in the nursery
rhyme that little boys are made of them ...... but, it doesn't say

that they eat them. Puppy dog's tails indeed ... no, nor slugs and snails either. Your Papa eats snails? Yes, I know but that's different ... I don't know why, but it just is. Now, try to be sensible and make up your mind ... blueberry jello? Okay, you've got it. We're getting somewhere at last. What else? .... a plate of chocolate cookies to yourself? Okay - now what do you want to drink? ... Now, don't be stupid, Jason. Little boys do not drink Jack Daniels - no, not even on the rocks. Now, what is it to be? Do you want? - Coke, Fanta, Seven - up? .... Jason, come out from under the table at once, do you hear me? ... No, you are not a little doggie drinking a bowl of water. You are a little boy and, without doubt, a very badly behaved little boy. Stop barking and get back on your chair at once ... oh, very well - anything for a quiet life. Young man, would you be so kind as to pick up this little doggie and put him back into his bed? ... You would? Great. .. Oh, Jason - you naughty, naughty little boy - this time you've gone too far. Stop growling and tell the waiter sorry you bit him or I'll take you back home directly. I just don't know how to apologise, young man. I sure am sorry. He's so highly strung, that's his problem .......
I'll pretend you didn't say that, Waiter. Now, please bring him a coke for his drink and we'll, leave it at that ... Jason, stop trying to balance that plate on the end of your nose and listen to me. ... Jason - now look what you've done - that's a plate and a cup and saucer I'll be expected to pay for. No, you cannot be a clown in a circus when you grow up. Indeed. I doubt if you'll live that long. I really do... Oh my, Jason, guess who's just come in ... no, it is not Yogi Bear. It's Mrs Brown from next door and little Penny. Isn't that swell? .. Jason, put your tongue back into your mouth this very moment. Hi. Louella! Hi Penny! Please come and join us. Great! Sit you down right there. Good, good. You sit next to me and Penny can sit there next to her little friend Jason, can't she? Fine, fine. Now, what brings you to town this afternoon, Louella? I thought .... Jason! Stop pushing Penny like that. Nice little boys do not push little girls like that. They have to be kind and loving

... Jason, stop hugging Penny like that. I said love not strangle! Ah, here's the waiter again for your order, I expect. We're having a flat white, a coke and two plates of chocolate cookies .... You'll have the same - are you sure? Right - the same it is, then, Waiter, thank you. And what about Penny? What would she like? .. Oh, dear, you feel sick, do you? Isn't that a shame? So you don't want anything at all? ... Only a knickerbocker glory with double nuts and cream and a raspberry smoothy. I see. Well, that should settle matters one way or the other, shouldn't it? Got it, Waiter? Right that's it, I guess. As I was saying, Louella .... Jason, stop putting spoons down the back of Penny's dress and go back to your seat at once and wait for you jello like a good boy. Right, that's better. ... No, Jason, I do not think Penny's dress looks sloppy. I think it's real cute. I just adore that little bow of ribbon on her ... Jason - leave that bow alone at once, do you hear me? ... I am so sorry, Louella, sometimes I don't believe that Jason and I live in the same world. I think ... Ah, here's the waiter with our order. I expect yours will be along directly. Thank you, Waiter. Thank you. That's great. Jason - you should wait until Penny has her tea before you start ... Are you sure, Louella? Okay - fine. Go for it then, Jason. What? Didn't I ask you if you wanted to go the bathroom before you came out? ... I don't care how urgent it is. You'll have to wait till we've all finished tea. Jason - stop slapping your jello with your spoon like that, I said stop it ... now, just look what you've done - there's a large piece of jello sliding down Mrs Brown's lovely white dress. That's the end. Leave the table at once and go and stand in that corner facing the wall. At once, I said. Louella, I'm lost for words, I just don't know how to apologise ... Jason! What are you doing in the corner. *(Rushes over left - calling)* Waiter, waiter, do you have a floor cloth and a mop .... ?

# TUESDAY

## Anne Barwood

"Billy, come on, boy" I yell. "Come on, boy." Billy suddenly halts, too quick for his body - back legs running smack into his front, his bottom rising skyward. He composes himself then sniffs the air as if my words are caught via smell rather than sound. His body turns away like a penny racer, tongue lopping from his mouth, the signal to start the charge. I take a step backward, not in fright, but to ground myself. He bounds across the field in eager anticipation of the treat he knows is his. Surprisingly, this is one of the few times he manages to pull himself short, instead of landing full force into my legs. He sits in front of me, head tilted to the side, still with tongue lolling as if the effort to place it back in his mouth could cause his early demise. Steam rises from his fur, evidence of a battle between his body heat and the sharp cold of this November morning. In order to reward my "Lovely" I have to do a macabre strip. It's my own fault for putting the dog biscuits in my shirt pocket. To get to my shirt, I first have to remove my top pair of gloves, the thermal lined, big, podgy black ones. I can keep the old woollen, fingerless green ones on. Then I undo my scarf, which is wrapped tightly around like a neck brace, next onto my big, cuddly padded jacket, followed, in quick succession, by my cosy quilted one. I now get down to my sweater, the one with Cardiff University on the front. (Not that I've ever been to Cardiff. I picked it up in a jumble sale for fifty pence) Then, Hallelujah! My shirt! The biscuits are removed sharpish, the rewind button pressed, and the clothes appear back on my, now slightly chilled body.

Billy sits patiently and reverently except for the slight uncontrollable bottom shuffle, like a child awaiting their Easter eggs. He knows the routine, the biscuit is the canine equivalent of half-time oranges, our steps will be retraced back home.

Jack the Postman is just walking down our drive, his routine as rigid as mine. It feels good to know the postman's name, as it becomes more personal a service. "Morning!" his usual greeting. "It's a bit parky this morning. Isn't it, love?" He says this looking at my 'Michelin Man' appearance, grinning. "Bet you're warm as toast in there! Peraps' I should try extra layers, not for warmth, just so as I bounce if I fall off me bike." Anything interesting 'post wise' today?" I ask hopefully but knowing the answer. "Looks just like the bills, love. Well - you know - brown envelopes!" I'm not sure if postmen have a delivery etiquette code. he never calls me by my name - always 'love' or 'pet' and always says the colour of the envelopes as if voicing "I don't look at people's post, but I know what the different colours are. " Got to go. No rest for the wicked!" his usual parting statement. He tousles Billy's fur, puts his left foot on the left pedal of his red Post Office issue bike and gives momentum with his right. The bike glides down the road like a Viking longboat with Jack at the helm. This lasts for about three seconds until he attempts to swing his right leg over the frame. At sixty-four, he's lost some of his lower flexibility. This noble vision changes into a Harold Lloyd scene as he wobbles and swerves out of view. I smile, bitter sweet, but still a smile. The hilarity of Jack's cycling proficiency intermingled with his loss of youth and impending retirement A sense of bereavement on his behalf, what do retired postmen do? I turn away with a wave, as every morning, not daring to watch any more in case something bad happens.

The door, a little stiff, gives entrance after a little personal persuasion. Mental note :- have door fixed at weekend. I've been noting the door mentally for months now. Urgent mental note:- remember mental notes!

Billy barges past straight to his water bowl, lapping its contents loudly, managing to get as much on the floor as his tongue. I flick the switch to both the kettle and the radio, as always, just in time for the 7-30am news bulletin of war, famine and desolation followed by the non-amusing. "amusing" story at the end Usually involving small, furry animals, great altitudes and needless tax expenditure. Sydney appears, as if from nowhere, wrapping herself around my legs in her "Breakfast please!" way. Sydney is our very 'unmale' ginger tomcat with ovaries instead of 'love spuds' - as John would say! "Hang on a second!" Whether she understands me or not, I don't know, but she does move away, giving me some room, but not too much just in case I forget her needs. I remove the tin from the cupboard and empty half into her bowl. She gives me an approving nod then digs in. I check her litter tray, clean up the debris, put more paper in the base and refill it. It amuses me about the paper. Self-important people photographed going about their 'so called' important business, thinking that these pictures will influence people's views and behaviour, when, in reality, their most common use is to shield people's floors from cat poop!

The click of the kettle tells me it's my turn. I wash my hands and pour boiling water into my cup. As usual, I have forgotten to buy milk, and I don't have it delivered any more so, yet again, I have it black. The travel report comes on the radio and I realise I am running late. I take the stairs two at a time, tearing off layers of clothes as I go. No time for a shower, hair tied back, tights, knee-length skirt, crispish white shirt, sensible shoes and fitted jacket - my work clothes. I charge back downstairs, kiss Billy and lock him in the kitchen, grab my briefcase, coat and post, then make my way to the station, trying to regain composure with every step.

The train hasn't arrived when I get to the station, so I stand in my usual spot, chosen because it gives a slight respite from the wind. I stand alone as an island, away from the groups of school-goers and the mobile obsessed. I feel calm beginning to flow over me, starting at the toes and rising through my abdomen.

"Well, look who it isn't!" A voice appears from my side. I turn to look at the mysterious speaker. It's our old next door neighbour, Jean (I think that was her name. ) "How are you? How's John?" She must have seen a slight twitch in my eye. "Oh. not with him any more? Better off, I'd say . Men, they're all the same - never grow up, only ever want their mothers, or you to become their mothers. You cook and clean up after them, and what thanks do you get? None. You give them the best of yourself and they toss you aside for a new model. Well, at least, you didn't have children. You didn't, did you? No. Anyway, plenty more fish in the sea, young girl like you. How's that dog of yours? Still got him playful like he was? Alan was saying, just the other day, how he wishes he hadn't moved - the garden was so much bigger. But, with his back, we had to have a bungalow 'cos, you know, it got too much for him." Thankfully the train pulled up and Jean scurried off to grab her seat - it was her right as an elderly lady. There wasn't a seat spare for me in the whole carriage, so that the whole journey was spent with an arm swinging above my head, swaying in time to the motion of the train, slightly hypnotic. I started to think about John, only natural really. He had wanted to have children, but I thought we were too young. Billy and Sydney were 'surrogate children,' or trial runs. If we could manage jobs, life and pets, then perhaps someday we may be able to manage children as well. He never once said I may have to manage without him. Thank heavens no babies on top of no John.

It is not so hard as I thought it was going to be. On my own. The food is always my choice and I can openly have as much chocolate, as I like, in the house. The house stays tidy for longer. Everything is exactly where I put it. There isn't as much washing up and no dirty wet towels are left on the bathroom floor! Every night, it's my choice on the television or radio. But there's no voice - just silence. Who's there to discuss the bad day at work or the funny little anecdote that made that day? When I watch the telly, I find myself turning to look at him, to see if he felt the humour or sadness in whatever is going on. And, at night, the extra warmth and comfort, found in our love and sharing is gone.

The train slows to stop at my destination. I step out of the carriage and start walking up the hill. I've not got to rush, my first appointment isn't till ten o'clock. I try to think about what I want for tea and if it will snow before Christmas. But Jean's "You're better without him" keeps filling my head. I walk through the gates, turn left, walk about fifty yards and stop. I rummage through my briefcase. "I'm not better. I miss you, John. Happy Birthday, angel." I place my card on his gravestone. Turn and head for work.

# POOR GEORGE

## Alfred J. Greenaway

*Miriam is boovering. After a moment or so, she stops, keeping her hands on the cleaner.*

I suppose people would think I was a bit peculiar if they knew, I love hoovering. I do the whole house every day - upstairs, downstairs, in my lady's chamber. It's nice to know the place is properly clean, but when I empty all that fluff out of the bag, I wonder if I've got any carpet left; but I can't stop it. And there's the exercise. It takes it out of me hauling the machine up and down stairs every day and pushing it around - but it saves the trouble of traipsing along to the 'Keep Fit' class. Besides, it makes me feel that I'm still one of the world's workers and not just a rotting vegetable. You don't feel so lonely, and I am, very lonely. Poor George! It's eighteen months now. I miss him dreadfully, but you have to put a brave face on it. Look on the bright side, that's my motto. *(After a pause)* After all, if he behaves himself, he'll get remission and he could be out in another six months - maybe sooner. Three years, that's what he got - for fraud. I don't know, I really don't, how he could be so dishonest. We didn't need the money. And what did he do with it? I never saw any of it. Horses, I suppose - unless he's got another woman tucked away somewhere. I don't think so. He'd look on it as an unnecessary expense. *(She sits)* We never had children. George said we couldn't afford them to begin with. We'd do better to build up a little capital first. But the years rolled by and it got too late. It's been a great sorrow to me, but I've never said. So all I've got now is George.

I've never been an enthusiastic churchgoer, but George said that making yourself known at church was good for business, so we became regulars. He even became a sidesman, until that fuss about the collection money. I never quite understood what that was all about, but George had a row with the Vicar and we've never been since. People seemed to avoid us after that. Not very Christian, I thought.

I write to him every week. He writes sometimes - usually when he wants something - like scented soap. Funny he should be so keen on scented soap, but he was always very fussy about personal hygiene. In his last letter, he said that you meet a very good class of person in prison these days. Makes you wonder what we've come to, doesn't it?

When he comes out, I don't want to put on a "holier than thou' attitude, so to form a sort of bond between us, I took up shop-lifting. I thought it might make him feel better if we were on the same level, so to speak. But I don't really like it. I'm not a dishonest person by nature. Mind you, it can be quite exciting and gives a sort of focus for the day. When you're as lonely as I am, you need some distraction. I've given it up now. I don't want to be 'inside' when he comes out. Anyway, I've got a larder crammed with food, and some of it must be past its sell-by date. One good thing, I've got a nice selection of scented soaps - He'll like that. *(Standing up)* Well, I'd best get on. There's still upstairs to do, and I don't want to be late for my elevenses. I have a mug of Nescafe and one digestive biscuit every morning at eleven sharp - on the dot. *(There is a knock on the door)* Who can that be? Double-glazing tout, I expect. Or could it be George? *(She hurries out)* George! George! I'm coming!

## BEST-SELLING BLUES
### Angeline Wilcox

*"Hell hath no fury like a woman scorned" - especially if, after a rather messy divorce, her husband then goes on to write a best-seller and reap the rewards of literary success. In an attempt to stem her fury, the woman scorned in this monologue makes a desperate phone call to her best friend.*

Miriam, it's me! Have you seen this morning's paper? The wretch has only gone and done it! He's number one on the best-sellers' list. Can you believe it? I'm livid! Well of course I'm talking about Colin, who else? No, Miriam, I will not calm down. Do you realise how it feels to see my bloody ex-husband making a success of his life after all that he's put me through? It's driving me mad. Every time I open a newspaper or walk past a bookshop, his silly face just leers at me as he clutches his precious volume in one hand and a glass of champagne in the other. Did you see him on "This Morning?" No, of course I don't usually watch it; I just happened to be in Currys and there he was - on every damn television in the shop. He's got a nerve! Do you know, he actually claims that he's doing for Portugal what Peter Mayle did for Provence? Talk about having an inflated opinion. No, I'm not jealous! How could I be jealous of that snivelling little toad with a personality bypass? What do you mean, "He has a certain boyish charm?" Oh please, Miriam, he has as much charm as a slug with halitosis. I don't care if he is the father of my children. That was bad timing on my part and a total misjudgement of his capabilities. All right, I might have seen something in him once, but that was during one of my weak and charitable moments 20 years ago. I was young and impressionable for heaven's sake. Don't laugh, Miriam, I haven't always been a ruthless and vindictive woman. Oh no, that began when voluptuous Venetia came on the scene. Trouble is, she's still there now and helping him spend his delightfully fat royalty cheques! No, it's not just the money, it's the principle. If it hadn't been for me, Colin would still be a second-rate computer programmer who played golf at the weekends. Let me remind you, Miriam, who was it who always enthused about holidays in Portugal? Who harboured the ambition to give up work, move out there and write a best-selling novel? And who went to creative writing classes so that one day she might be able to fulfil this dream? Yes, Miriam, it was me! And now look at what my ex-husband has done. First he has an affair with a bimbo young enough to be his daughter, second, they buy a beach bar on the Algarve, and then he discovers that despite mindlessly fingering computer keyboards for 25 years, he is able to string together something resembling a sentence. Finally, he enrols on a pathetic correspondence course entitled "Naughty Novel-writing for Novices" and, hey-presto, Colin Carterton becomes a literary legend. I could just about cope with him finding another woman, but when it comes to stealing my creative ideas, that is just too much! What do you mean, I should have kept my ideas to myself ? We shared a bed for 20 years and we had to find some stimulating topic of conversation to pass the time. And that's another thing, he certainly didn't base the carnal activities of his characters on his life with me. He must have been inspired by his more athletic amorous adventures with Venetia! No, Miriam, I am not hurt, just bitter! Yes, it's a shame I couldn't have "beaten him to it" as you so kindly put it. No doubt, had I found myself a sugar daddy instead of marrying Colin, bringing up two children, running a home and working full time, I could have written a best-seller. However, in our marriage, fate dealt me the cruel blow and here I am, the faithful former wife, left to cope with two adolescent sons who are both going through a virility crisis. It's not funny, Miriam. They've read their father's book and think they're missing out because they don't have loin-shattering experiences with pouting blonde caddies in the back of a golf buggy. It seems that a hole-in-one has a very different meaning according to their father! Of course, they think Colin's wonderful now. He's gone from being "sad" to "cool". They want to spend their summer holidays with him for the first time in five years. It's amazing what 400 pages of fornicating on the fairway can do for your popularity - and your bank balance! Do you know, Miriam, there's all that beautiful Portuguese countryside and he never even mentions it. The only way you can tell the wretched book is set in Portugal is because all the characters end up bonking in sun-kissed golf bunkers, or scoffing freshly caught sardines in the clubhouse. No, Miriam, I did not find the incident beneath the golfing umbrella with Carlos the pro and Atlanta the trainee caddy rather exciting. Honestly, I'm surprised at you! I thought you had a more discerning literary palate. What do you mean, you thought it was a "jolly good holiday romp"? You make it sound like Jilly Cooper let loose on a package tour. Well, yes, I have read it, but it was only from a critical point of view. You must understand that, Miriam. Heaven knows, I didn't want to read it. Quite frankly, I found the whole book disgusting and very badly written. No, Miriam, he didn't send me a signed copy. Well, how should I know if he's going to write a blessed sequel! Look, Miriam, it's me you're meant to be interested in, not him. I am your best friend, you should be sympathising with me. If you're so interested in Colin's writing career, then why don't you fly out to the Algarve and visit him? What do you mean "Funny you should say that"? Miriam? Miriam? Talk to me! ..... You're doing what? .... Oh, Miriam, how could you?

# A SHELTERED LIFE
## Brian J. Burton

*An elderly lady is sitting, well wrapped up, on a bench centre stage. She glances up to the sky.*

Oh dear, it doesn't look as if it's going to give up. This is the third day running I've sat here in this shelter with the rain pouring down all afternoon. It's as black as night out there and it's only just after three. One of the dark days before Christmas; that's what my late husband used to say. It's bad enough sitting here with the rain, but that hole in the roof up there doesn't help I've lost count of the number of times I've rung that man in the office but nothing's been done about it - nothing at all. I bet they'll do something about it when the season starts and the visitors come here in their thousand. Probably won't be raining then and it won't matter. Mind you, used to have rain from time to time in the summer, when we came here as visitors on a regular basis. Before we moved here for good, that was. But not like it is now, in the winter like. And the wind doesn't help. Cuts though you like a knife, it does. Mind you, my Charlie did say it might not be as nice here in the winter as it is in the summer. Stands to reason, that does. I understand that no, but I took no heed of what Charlie said at the time. But he turned out to be right as usual Arthur and Madge didn't take much notice of what he said either. We were all that keen to sell up and live here for good when we retired - all four of us. It seems years and years since we first met Madge and Arthur down here - by the kiosk on the bowling green My Charlie asked Arthur if he fancied a game and that was it. Hit it off from the start, we did. For nigh on twenty years we came down here and met them, at the back end of July. Always stayed at the same boarding house - guest houses, they call 'em now. We were regular members of the bowls club in the summer. We never saw them in the winter, of course. Wrote, of course, at Christmas and birthdays. As I recall, it was Madge who first put forward the idea that we might sell up and come and all live here when we retired. As I said, Charlie wasn't too keen on the idea, in the first place, but he came round to it in the end  So, sold our house, we did and  came here to Walton-on-Sea for good. Innocents  abroad, we were - all four of us. Hadn't thought it through properly, we were so obsessed with the notion. Seemed like a paradise - a chance to start life all over again, And Arthur and Charlie, bless 'em, like brothers they were. *(After a long pause)* Both gone now - both of  them. Strange how neither of them lasted very long after we moved down here *(After a pause)* I reckon  they missed  their mates back home down at the pub. In fact, I know they did. *(Pause)*   So did I too, to tell you the truth.  I sometimes play with the idea of going back to where I used to live but the I realise that most of my friends back there are probably  gone by now, I stopped hearing from them years back, I did. Anyway, I couldn't afford it, if I did. And I sold all the furniture when I moved into the unit. Oh, I've got a bit in the building society but not much. Living in that unit isn't cheap, by any means. Oh, look, I do believe the sun's going to come out. There's a bit of blue up there in the sky - almost enough to make a sailor a pair of trousers, as my Charlie used to say - bless him. It won't be long now before Spring's here and all those daffodils by the Concert Hall will be coming out. Yes, the rain's stopped - just in time for Madge to turn up, as she does every afternoon, in time for us to go to the Ivy Tea rooms and have a nice cup of tea. I don't know what I'd do without her, I really don't. She's got this little part-time job at the cleaners. I couldn't work, because of my blood pressure. Ah, here she is. Hello, Madge, did you have a good day at the shop? You must tell me all about it when we're having our tea.  No, I've been fine. Just sitting here, you know, and thinking about the old days. *(Rising and moving left* Come on then, Madge, love, let's get cracking, as my Charlie used to say - bless him - let's get cracking.

# SUMMER SCHOOL
## Angela Lanyon

Oh, here you are, Nancy, and you managed to get a table. No, don't look at my hair - it's a wonder it hasn't all fallen out after last week. Now, just let me get myself settled - and coffee. Just what I needed, and I must tell you, before we start, that you were absolutely right not to go to the conference this year. Everything people told you about about St Polycarp's was absolutely right. The food was dreadful - school dinners, if you know what I mean. No imagination. And miles of corridors. Even Jackie said - do you remember Jackie? Oh, you must do, she was the one with the pink hair who made such a dead set at Clive. Of course you remember. That lecturer, the one who was talking about Jane Austen - nearly drove him bonkers with her silly questions. And, of course, that woman from Southport was there again, and Brian - with yet another suitcase of eye-blinding socks. Brian. I said to him, why don't you go for something more restrained? I mean, Day-Glo socks and sandals at sixty something, I ask you - and that dreadful tie that lit up when you pressed it. What do you mean, what was I doing pressing Brian's chest? I slipped. No, in the dining room and no, I hadn't had anything to drink, well not then, Though, I can tell you, I did later and I wasn't the only one. Two or three of us - Marcia - you remember Marcia - she had that sort of thing about Hemmingway and stuck up a whole lot of posters in her room. Oh, what? Geoff- oh, yes Geoff was there again, full flow, my dear, as always and so pompous - I'm sure that wife of his must be stone deaf or she wouldn't put up with it all - yes, that's right, that stringy little woman, always looks as though she's wearing a damp dishcloth. We did Tennyson, of course, and I must say I got carried away with all that Arthurian stuff. 'Lo the level lake and the long glories of the winter moon' And the lecturer, such a gorgeous man, I must tell you. Quite fell for him - tall and very romantic looking - He kept calling me his dear Vivian - no I don't think he meant I was an old witch, though, if he took a look at my hair now, he might think so. Of course, you can imagine Jackie's reaction, you know how fraught she gets if she sees anything tasty slipping from her grasp. God, I mean, is that woman predatory ... "Oh, Campbell, darling" - and at breakfast and it wasn't as if she knew him from Adam when she arrived. Of course, I rose above all that - for the most part, my dear, but I did get just the teeniest bit put out when she came round when we were all having a tea break and asking what I suppose she thought were erudite questions. I'd have thought she could see the poor man wanted a breather, but she was so persistent. Of course, I did my best to deflect her, but in the end, he just stood up and stalked off - just like that. Of course, the rest of us of us were open mouthed and Brian said - purple socks, my dear, with orange spots - Brian said hadn't she read the course books before she came. Well, you can imagine. She flew off the handle and said she was only trying to get her money's worth and that's what the lecturers were for and Carys - no, you won't know Carys. I think she's Welsh or something - petite and very dark - you'd have liked her - great sense of humour - she was always in a fit about something - we used to giggle away like mad. Fifth Form at Malory Towers - you know, Enid Blyton - I always think it's a bit like school - cocoa after lights out, only in our case it was gin in a tooth glass. And then, of course, there was this expedition to the different sites and naturally Jackie held everything up leaving her sunglasses in the loo at Avebury and we all had to wait while she went and looked for them. And then, Campbell had to go and look for her. Took absolutely ages, and Carys and I were in the back of the bus just bursting with curiosity when they eventually got back on and, of course, we were late and it meant a frightful scramble to get ready for dinner. Well, there was this sort of impromptu party - dressing up - it's a sort of new thing - I don't know really whether I liked the idea or not, but Jackie naturally behaved as if it was put on for her benefit and had so many scarves and things you'd think it was the dance of the seven veils, never mind Camelot. Actually, I thought it was a pity she let her hair down - you could see all the roots and I mean if people are going to go around pretending to be younger than they are, they really ought to try to be convincing - though I must admit she's got a good figure for her age. Couldn't help but see it, could I, not after she stripped off and went into the lake. I really thought Brian's socks would burst into flames with the excitement, but I must admit he turned up trumps. Threw off his sandals and dived in as if he'd been doing it all his life. Came up. clutching Jackie with one arm and waving the other and shouting Excalibur! Things got a bit confused after that, my dear, but he turned up at breakfast looking quite pinky and perky. Poor Campbell looked daggers drawn so maybe Carys was right when she said Jackie and he had a thing going. Incidentally, she told me, in the strictest confidence, that Brian was quite high up in the civil service. I suppose that explains the socks.

# SUPERMARKET BLUES
## Alfred J. Greenaway

*Enter a shopper with a shopping trolley and a wire basket on top*

How do you get on with supermarket trolleys? The stupid things always seem to have one wheel which wants to go off in a different direction from the other three: or the brakes lock and you can't move the blessed thing at all. They seem to have a will of their own and wherever you want to go, they don't. Modern technology can put a man on the moon or have him go for a spacewalk, but can't come up with the perfect supermarket trolley. That's why I bring my own and balance one of their wire things on the top. Funny places, supermarkets, when you look around. Can anyone tell me why so many junior managers wear suits too big for them? Perhaps it's because they're so junior they have to allow for growing. And another thing, why are they always moving things around? I think they do it for a bit of a giggle. There's nothing like the bemused look on the face of an old lady who goes to pick up a pint of milk only to find that she's looking at a display of boot polish. They're into cut flowers and pot plants now. I went into one store recently and there was a large mound of greenery, looking like an arrangement for an elaborate funeral. I asked one of the girls who was under that lot - the manager? All she said was "soree." And I said, "Well yes, I suppose we all are, but never mind, you carry on with your shelf-filling.: She gave me a funny look and disappeared round the corner, muttering. There's a lot of interest to be had at the checkout, of course. Have you counted the number of times, you've arrived there, after carefully weighing up which is the fastest queue,when the girl decides it's her coffee break or the till roll runs out, or the woman in front of you has fifteen coupons that have to be checked. It's a natural law. Some people have a name for it. To help pass the time, I look at other people's trolleys and try to guess their life style. For instance, six bottles of spring water and a lettuce. Someone on a diet, hoping forlornly to get back to the shape she was in her heyday? Or could she be a reformed alcoholic - who keeps a rabbit. Then there's the little old lady with just one item - a bottle of elder flower cordial. She doesn't need anything really; she's just come for an outing and a bit of a chat perhaps. I'm thankful I'm not behind that trolley piled high - mostly convenience foods - piloted by a young flibbertigibbet with a harassed look. Rich man's darling? He has half a dozen kids by his previous marriages. They take a lot of feeding and she can't cook, so it's the freezer and convenience packs. What's on top of that pile? A bottle of disinfectant? Ah ha! She's had enough and plans to lace his whisky with it, and end this gilded drudgery. I can guess what you're thinking. The woman's off her trolley! Well, yes and no, but it helps to pass the time. Isn't anyone going to ask what I've got in my trolley? Well, I'll tell you anyway. Some smoked salmon, a lemon and a bottle of plonk on special offer. No, I'm not entertaining a fancy man. I'll let you into a secret - it's my birthday, and I'm going to have a party all on my own It does you good to make a fuss of yourself, even if it's only once a year. It's my turn now - by - ee!

## YOU HAVE BEEN WARNED
### Brian J. Burton

*This is based on an event which happened during a coach tour to Russia. The tour guide - a charming, educated lady who hailed from St Petersburg - had a delightful sense of humour and punctuated her warning with infectious laughter*

Now, ladies and gentlemen, if I can have your attention for a few minutes. Already, we are approaching our destination for the day and our hotel for tonight - our hotel for tonight. And you must be tired after your long journey. Of course you are, aren't you? There are things I have to tell you about the hotel. The owners of this hotel have gone to a great deal of trouble trying to bring it up to a high European standard. They aim to make it the best hotel in the town. Of course, it is the only hotel in the town. No, but seriously, there are certain things I have to tell you about the hotel - about the hotel. First of all, there is the bathroom. There is a glass shelf over the washbasin. Whatever you do, you must not put anything at all on it - nothing at all - not even a toothbrush. (*Starts to laugh*) But seriously, It may well collapse and fall off the wall. Now about the toilet seat. It is some distance from the toilet roll holder, so I suggest that you plan your journey very carefully and be well-prepared - well prepared. (*Laughing*) If you decide to take the toilet roll with you to the toilet seat, be very careful not to drop it as the floor is sloping and the toilet roll will run away from you. (*Laughing*) Now - the towel -already you will find that there are proper towels.When we first visited this hotel, guests asked me why there were only tea towels in the bathroom. *(Laughing)* This I managed to have changed , after many letters to the management, and even threatening not to stay at their hotel in future, but already there are proper towels. Now, the hot water - you may find that you have to run the shower for a very long time to get any hot water and even then, it will not be hot. You must be patient, very patient - yes. And the hook on the back of the bathroom door - do not hang your dressing gown on it or the hook will probably fall off the door. *(Laughing)* Now about the bedroom. There is no air conditioning and the windows are sealed. However, there is one little window, high up, which will open to give you some air. But seriously, be very, very careful about reaching it. There is a chair in the room which is very sturdy. So stand on this chair and, then put your feet on the television table but be very careful not to knock the television onto the floor. *(Laughing)* It has happened - has happened. Then reach up to the little window and pull it towards you. But, whatever you do, do not push it, or it will fall out into the street - into the street below. *(Laughing)* Oh, and I forgot to tell you, be careful with the handle on the shower. It may come away in your hand. *(Laughing )* No, seriously, be warned - it does. Already we are at the hotel so you will be able to get some rest, of course. And please do not forget, cases outside your doors at 6-30 in the morning. We have a long journey tomorrow, of course - a long journey tomorrow.-

# A RING O'ROSES

### Alfred J. Greenaway

*The Reception area in the offices of a suburban solicitors' firm. Rose, the receptionist sits behind the switchboard. She wears a headset. It is Monday morning. She dials a number and waits.*
Bessie? It's me ..... Rose ..... Hi! ..... Did you have a good weekend? ..... Really? ..... Really? ..... You didn't? ..... You did! Well, I'm .....

Hang on ..... Fogarty, Docherty, Dwindle and Pine. Can I help you? Pardon? ..... Yes, I suppose it does sound a bit like a nursery rhyme. I never thought of that. How can I help you? ..... Mr Fogarty. I'm afraid that's not possible. Mr Fogarty is no longer with us. ..... No, I can't say where he's gone . He's passed on, you see ..... Well. I suppose you could put it like that ..... Yes, that's right, he's dead, but he was a very elderly gentleman and it was sometime ago now..... I'll put you through to Mr Doherty, he's still very spry - for his age. Hold the line, please. .... No, I won't give you a burst of muzak. We're far too old-fashioned to go in for gimmicks like that. I'm sorry, Mr Docherty's line is engaged. I'll put you through as soon as possible ...... Bessie? You still there? Some old dear says we sound like a nursery rhyme - Fogarty, Docherty, Dwindle and Pine. I suppose she's got a point there. I say it so many times a day, I don't listen to it. Where were we? Ah, yes, the weekend. Glad you had a good time ..... Well, on Saturday I went to "Four Weddings and a Funeral." ..... What do mean, I couldn't have? ...... Don't be daft. I went to the flicks to see that old film "Four Weddings and a Funeral." I missed it the first time round ...... It's good ...... You should see it. Hang on. A Mrs Lively would like to speak to you,sir. I'm putting you through now, madam. Fogarty, Docherty, Dwindle and Pine ...... I'm sorry, you've got the wrong number ...... Well, it's not my fault, is it?. You dialled. I didn't ...... Bessie? That was some idiot complaining because I'm not British Gas! Some people! Where were we? ...... oh, yes - at the flicks. I'd dolled myself up, just to please me. Well, you never know! And I happened to sit next to this fellow - well dressed  - blazer - light trousers - smart shoes. A neat little moustache and beautiful teeth. They must have cost a bomb. Ever so polite. We got into conversation and the upshot is he's invited me to dinner at *The Drunken Duck* next Saturday ...... Well. I...... Hang on .. Fogarty, Doch..... Oh., it's you, Mrs Dwindle ...... No, I'm afraid he's out ..... I don't know. About an hour, expect...... I'll tell him you called. Bye..... Bessie. That  was Mrs Dwindle.  She doesn't trust poor old Fatty. She's always checking up on him. Can't imagine what mischief she thinks he'll get up to, not with women, anyway. I was telling you about my new friend. He's a lovely talker. Mind you, I've a nasty suspicion he might be married. He has that mildly repressed look that most married men have. Or could he be a con man? But you can't say "no" to a free dinner, can you? ...... Yes, I know there's no such thing as a free lunch, or a free dinner, come to that, but don't worry, I can look after myself ...... Yes, I'll try to remember everything me mum told me. ...... I'll give you a ring next Monday to let you know how I got on, unless he turns out to be white slaver, or whatever they call 'em now, and ships me off to South America! ..... Thanks ..... Fogarty, Docherty, Dwindle and Pine. Can I help you?

## SALLY BROWN

### A Blitz Ballad
### Brian J. Burton

*During the Second World War, a very popular radio comedian, Nosmo King (Jack Watson) always ended his act with a monologue - almost always a highly sentimental patriotic call of some kind. The following monologue, in a similar doggrel style, is intended as a tribute to a now half-forgotten entertainer who coined his stage name from a notice in a railway carriage - No Smoking.*

She worked in Lyons Teashop
And her name was Sally Brown.
I daresay you'd have seen her
If you'd ever lunched in town.
She wasn't much to look at -
Quite ordinary and plain,
Like a thousand other women
That one meets upon life's lane.
Her world was unexciting -

She did nothing very well,
Like so many other people
Who fail to ring the bell.
And then came the September
Of Nineteen - Thirty-Nine,
That changed the life of everyone
Including yours and mine.
She felt she must do something
To help to win the war,
So she joined the ranks of A.R.P.
For full-time, what is more.
She learned to drive an ambulance,
Wore a uniform of blue,
And waited, waited, waited
For something more to do.
But the days and and days of waiting,
Made a fog of Sally's brain
And she wished she was a waitress
Back in Civvy Street again.
Then one evening, with the others,
She was sitting round the fire,
Playing cards to pass the time away -
Even that began to tire -
When she heard the sirens wailing
And the distant sound of guns
And the purring of the engines
Of the fast approaching Huns.
She sprang to Action Station -
How mechanical by now -
And she waited for her orders
Amidst that booming row.
Then the call came to her station
That the bombs had found their mark,
So she took her wheel and started off

Careering through the dark.
All the town seemed to be burning
Like one fire from end to end.
In and out the burning buildings,
Her way she had to wend.
Till , at last, she found her target
A giant City store
Where the flames were leaping skyward,
Like so many, many more.
She dragged to safety all she could
Before she must retire
For the flames had overcome them
And her clothes were all on fire.
There isn't much to tell now
For Sally died that night -
She died from burns she'd suffered
When her clothes were set alight.
But she got her load to hospital,
That much we can relate.
She did her duty bravely
In spite of cruel fate.

She worked in Lyons Teashop
And her name was Sally Brown.
I daresay you'd have seen her
If you'd ever lunched in town.
But she's typical of all of them
All those Sally Browns
In our cities and our villages,
Our hamlets and our towns.
Let us drink a toast together -
A toast that is their due -
To the women of Great Britain
Who have proved themselves so true.

# HANBURY PLAYS

## MONOLGUES AND DUOLOGUES

# FURTHER TITLES AVAILABLE

## SINGULARLY SPEAKING
by
**Angeline Wilcox**
*Wide-ranging monologues for women of all ages*
ISBN:- 185205 2430

## LINES OF COMMUNICATION
by
**Brian J. Burton**
*15 duologues covering a wide range of subjects*
ISBN:- 185205 073X

## TWO CHARACTER COMEDY SKETCHES
by
**Susan Stepp**
*Ten hilarious sketches for student actors*
ISBN:- 185205 2554

## STORYTIME MONOLOGUES
by
**Larry Hillhouse**
*Ten updated fairy tales - comedy spoofs for all ages*
ISBN:- 185205 1639

# SHORT TWO-CHARACTER COMEDY SKETCHES
by
**Kirk Buis**
*Ten comedy sketches for mixed casts*

ISBN:- 1852052619


# COMEDY SCENES FOR TEENS
by
**Laurie Allen**
*Comic twists on the anxieties of being a teenager*

ISBN:- 1852052460


# COMEDY DUETS  no 2
by
**Peggy Kehert**
*Three outrageous updated fairy tale duets*

ISBN:- 1852051418


# COMEDY DUETS no 5
by
**Steve Wadleigh**
*Five more outrageous sketches for two players*

ISBN:- 1852052597


# FOR FURTHER DETAILS OF THESE TITLES
# VISIT OUR WEBSITE ON
# www.hanburyplays.co.uk